The Ocean Inside Kenji Takezo

DATE DUE

PITT POETRY SERIES

Ed Ochester, *Editor*

R

■ THE OCEAN INSIDE KENJI TAKEZO

RICK NOGUCHI

UNIVERSITY OF PITTSBURGH PRESS

This book is the winner of the 1995 Associated Writing
Programs' award series in poetry. Associated Writing Pro-
grams, a national organization serving over 150 colleges
and universities, has its headquarters at George Mason
University, Tallwood House, Mail Stop 1E3, Fairfax, Va.
22030.

Published by the University of Pittsburgh Press, Pittsburgh,
Pa. 15260
Copyright © 1996, Rick Noguchi
Manufactured in the United States of America
Printed on acid-free paper
10 9 8 7 6 5 4 3 2 1

Library of Congress Cataloging-in-Publication data and
acknowledgments are located at the end of this book.

A CIP catalog record for this book is available from the
British Library.

For Hiroshi and Emiko Noguchi, Deneen Jenks,

Steve Noguchi, and Rachel Ono

Surfers as a rule

do not like to talk surfing

to nonsurfers.

—*Phil Edwards*

▮CONTENTS

ONE

Wherever Kenji Takezo goes
He must surf
The perfect ride
In things that aren't waves.
This, the way he sees, is how
He survives, barely,
The world in which his balance is in
Constant peril. Last June
Kenji stood shirtless
After pedaling twice and gaining
Enough momentum on a blue Schwinn Cruiser.
He rode the Thirty-sixth Street Hill
Goofyfoot: right toes forward
Curling the handlebars,
Left ball planted on the seat.
He cut curb to curb,
Dodging parked cars,
Leaning and controlling each turn
Until he gathered too much
Velocity. Kenji developed speed wobbles.
Losing briefly his style.
But he continued to surf
The entire block,
The first person to go
Its length.
He then dumped the bike on the flats
Sliding after slamming
His belly against the asphalt.
He struggled to save the breath
That was knocked out of his lungs,
Even though the largest wave ever
Was not coming to drown him.

Kenji Takezo feels everybody
Watching him,
It is the biggest wave all day.
On a shortboard, he stands,
Cuts left.
Instead of doing the quick
Vertical maneuvers
Expected of him,
He borrows an old trick,
Makes it his.

He drops around his ankles
The trunks
His mother bought him
Last year for his birthday,
Exposing his private
Skin tone, the same color
Under his wristwatch.

The trunks at his ankles
Lose their purpose and become
Something else. Cuffs, binders,
Keeping his feet
Together, Siamese twins.
He cannot take the stance
Which would give him
The balance,
Enough to ride the wave's length.
He falls.

During the tumble, the wash of ocean,
The trunks are lost,
His feet twisting out of them,
Talents of an escape artist

He never practiced, never dreamed.
A sleight of the hand, a sleight of foot,
That surprises him.

The crowd, laughing,
Waits to cheer him.
But Kenji stays in the shallows
Planning his next trick.
He makes the best of it,
Paddles back out,
Catches another wave, then another,
Until the crowd grows
Tired of him and forgets.

▌Hunting for Grunion

The time my parents woke me
Near midnight, the moon was consuming itself.
I was a child
Who knew the days grew longer in June.
We drove to Malaga Cove
Where the ocean joined the dark sky.

Mother carried me,
Dead weight in her
Arms, across a stretch of soft sand.
My forehead in her neck, I felt
Her pulse giving me life.
Behind us, father swung
A propane lamp in one hand,
A metal bucket in the other.
I watched our shadow skip in front of us,
Never straying too far.

Mother and I sat on the cool shoreline
Watching father hurry,
Barefoot, between breakers.
After the water retreated,
He rushed out to grab with his hands
A silver fish thrashing
The exposed sea bottom,
Then raced back before the ocean returned.

He showed us in the bucket
Five creatures frightened by our curious faces.
Later, he scooped a glass jar full of wet sand.
When he held it to the light,
I don't recall seeing it,
But something was alive.

▌ Craving the Taste of Ocean

Kenji Takezo steals after breakfast
When his mother is not watching
The saltshaker from the kitchen table
Slipping it into his pants pocket
Simple as that.
All day he will sprinkle into his mouth
White granules of memory,
The residue of summer.

He acquired this habit,
This tickling on his tongue of crystals
Dissolving in saliva, after swallowing a wave.
His stomach just big enough to hold it.
Lifeguards pulled him from the water,
Gave him mouth to mouth,
And tried to rescue the wave.
But he refused to give it up.

At home he discovered too late
It could not be unswallowed.
He spewed his lunch then his dinner.
The wave would not come out. That night
The tide, full in his belly,
Shifted as he slept. Fever caused
The fluids in his body to swell.
He felt hot, cold,
Hot, until the wave collapsed inside him.
He woke in the damp shallows of his bed,
Gasping and thirsty for salt.

▌The Breath He Holds

It's the only thing Kenji Takezo does
Better than his brother Joe.
At last year's town competition
Kenji stayed under longest
Defeating Joe
And the six-year champ
Jack Sullivan who withdrew
After taking water in
Through the nose.

The family trophy case
Now displays the Steel Lung.
Kenji's the youngest
Ever to win it.
His parents are proud
He has such a knack,
That there is something
He can do besides surf.

To properly defend his title
This year, they purchase for him
A wooden vat,
Fix it in the rich soil
To stand near the older son's
Award-winning herb garden.
Hose water instead of wine
Fills it.

Kenji practices his technique
Back there twice a day
Before surfing and after school.
Saffron, sage, and basil
The last scents he breathes
Sinking down to sit

Cross-legged on the bottom,
A ten-pound brick in his lap,
Bubbles popping over his head,
No words inside them.
Nothing better on television
The neighbors come to watch him
Train until his skin becomes old.

▮ The Brother, Joe Takezo,
an Amateur Bodybuilder
Who Tries to Surf, Sometimes

He cannot move
The ocean
When he paddles.
It is too heavy.
Joe has the strength,
Can lift over his head
His own weight doubled.
But the water is not
So heavy.

Too much muscle, too much bulk,
His arms
He can't bend them
Far enough to relieve
The itch on his shoulders.
His strokes are short.
Not the long
Pull of a power lifter.
If they are strides
They are those of a child,
The steps of a young Kenji
Who paddles past him.

The ocean holds Joe up,
Keeps him
Inside the impact zone.
The waves there
Break on his head.
The strength of twice his weight
And more, the concussion
He once suffered
When the barbell
Slipped from his grip.

Overnight three holes the size of large fists appear in the front lawn. The father, up to get the morning newspaper, is first to discover them, and instantly becomes furious. For years he has prided himself on maintaining the neighborhood's most thriving nile green lawn.

Nobody burrows my grass and gets away with it, he says to himself, and returns inside, forgetting the newspaper, to wake up the son.

Get dressed and meet me out front, he says. The son, half asleep, does as told.

See those holes, the father says, whatever dug them may still be down there. We're going to flush it out.

The father uncoils the garden hose and shoves it deep into a hole. He steps back near the son standing with closed eyes, and turns the faucet on full blast. After a few minutes water floods out of the three holes, and nothing more.

Whatever was down there is now drowned, the father says to himself.

Taking soil from the empty flower bed, he packs the muddy holes, and reseeds. In a few weeks, he is sure, the lawn will be mended, greener than ever.

That evening the father falls asleep with ease, dreams about a prairie dotted with golden poppies. He is ready to run across it naked when a sharp, hissing cry of an alert tomcat wakes him. He hurries to the bedroom window, scans the backyard landscape deepened by night.

▌ El Toro del Mar

Warm Santa Ana winds,
I paddle into the wrecked
Mexican fishing boat.
A storm, winters ago,
Slammed it against the coral reef
Outside the bay.
Entering through the gash,
An incoming tide
Slaps shallow,
Vibrating the steel shell.

Those tossed overboard
Swam far enough away
To avoid being sucked under,
Only to drown later
From pure exhaustion.

On its side, the ship
Beached itself on Ynez's Point.
Overhead, light from a partial moon
Brightens the innards.
There is nothing here but kelp.
Exiting out the galley,
I wake a sea otter.
It coughs at me, and disappears.
My heart quickens.
A groundswell from a decaying hurricane
Starts drumming the hull faster.
Paddling toward shore,
I look back,
Trace the half-submerged craft
Against the night. Beneath me
The dark ocean beginning to stir.

After Kenji Takezo Loses His Trunks
His Appetite Is Met, Almost

For the first time he does not crave
The taste of ocean,
Something so salty
It leaves him
Thirsty for more waves.
He wants instead sweetness,
A flavor that punctuates
A good supper. He eats
Vanilla ice cream, his favorite.
He loves
The way it curls
When spooned out of the carton,
How its form disappears,
Melts into a calm sea,
Not the turbulent wash
That stole his trunks
Earlier that day, but the smooth
Morning after a storm.
He drinks from the bowl
Filling his empty stomach.
There, at the bottom, for a moment,
He thinks he sees his trunks
Floating in the tide going out.

■ The Second Oldest Balancing Butsumyo
Retired from the Circus, Age Twenty-three

He thought
He had balance.
His father
Trained him on the practice line
Since his second birthday.
His whole life
He walked
The drunk test
Successfully more hours
Than he slept.
Even then, he dreamt
Each foot's placement.
The high wire became his
Very long foot.

The circus stopped
In Redondo Beach.
He tried surfing.
He knew
How to balance on
A single object—
To balance on three objects
Moving at once
Was not possible.
He was determined to master it,
Make the board,
The wave, the ocean his
Very wide feet.

Mornings, he practiced.
The water at its calmest
Wobbled as land does
Under a gin drinker.

He had no feet.
Each time he fell,
The ocean caught him
Spun him
A moment longer
Than he thought comfortable.
The water became the net
Saving him from the hard surface of earth.
But it did not bounce him
Promptly back onto his feet.
The ocean with its very strong arms
Kept him under,
Tangled him in its triangular mesh.

He surfaced always
Greedy for air, the beach
Not where he left it.

I, the Neighbor Mr. Uskovich, Watch Every Morning Kenji Takezo Hold His Breath

Sometimes he will break
His concentration
And wave to me in a motion
Labored by water.
Bubbles, pouring out
His nostrils, much bigger
Than those in champagne
Opened to toast a new marriage.
He's only been under a few minutes
Today. I don't speak
Where he can see me,
Keep my thoughts to myself.
That Kenji cannot hear
The world, and the quick
Movement of lips
Frightens him.

The first time he saw
Someone speak
Words that weren't there,
He gasped
Inhaling his lungs full of water.
I was present when Mas,
The boy's father, found him.
He thought at first
His son was asleep,
Then that something was wrong.
He reached in hooking the boy
Under his arm to pull him from the vat.
But the fifteen-pound brick
That keeps Kenji submerged
Weighted him too well.

Mas in an act of love
Jumped in and lifted
His son high over his head.
I took the boy myself,
Carried him to the ground.
I put him in the basil plants.
Mas immediately started jabbing
His open palms into Kenji's belly
Driving out the water
That choked him.
In this way and on this morning
In this bed
He gave his son life.

▌ The Explosion at the Power Plant
Was Not a Supernova

Dusk is a minute late.
I watch it
Submerge. Once, as a child,
Mother left me

In a dark tub of lukewarm water.
I didn't move,
Took short breaths
The minute
She was gone.

If the puzzle that stars construct
Shatters, the universe,
I am told,
Will divide along invisible lines,
Will shift across the sky.
I believe it,

I also believe transmission wires
Sing the hollow
Music of ghost cicadas.
Picture this: the widow Sata,
Next door, climbing a mulberry tree,
Hangs her laundry
Off empty branches.

It's mid-noon and the flag's dead.

She experiences, momentarily,
Mild vertigo
Embraces a limb
Tighter than she's ever held

Her husband. Her clothes,
Right now, are clusters
Of purple fruit
Couched in night's pale dose.

Mother returned
Holding paraffin candles,
Flames igniting her smile.
I remember the walls,
A new stain of orange,

Stumbling like shadows.
I never slept cleaner.
When electricity was restored,
The lights, the television,
The time came to life in a flash.

▌The Madonna

He had workers
Install the cement
Fountain on the front lawn.
The family watched
Two days embarrassed.
Then, a stream of water
Spilling from the naked woman's
Pursed lips.
What did the neighbors think?
The family
Planned an abduction,
Would leave
No ransom note.
She had been taken by God.
Then, the phone calls
Claiming the eight-foot-tall woman,
Arms outstretched, had delivered
A forgotten warmth
Back to the neighborhood.
People visited from across
The city.
The father loved
Meeting them:
The man who traveled
Thirty miles on foot
To rub water into his face
Scarred by a chemical fire.
Out there now, a woman
Splashes at her genitals.
She is hoping for a miracle.

▊ His the Ocean

School did not teach Kenji Takezo
What he wanted to learn
How to read
The ocean, literature
That moved him for the first time.
Thousands of waves,
He studied
The way they broke
Sweeping left or right, often
Folding all at once.
The ones with form
Reminded him of his teacher
Ms. Scroggins. If she graded him
On what he knew about the surf
His report card would show
An A.

Then his parents would be proud.
They would let Kenji
Surf as much as he wanted.
In fact they would encourage him,
Tell their son
Keep up the good work,
Reward him with a new surfboard.
But Ms. Scroggins did not know
He had the power to forecast
A rise in the ocean.

▌ The Really Long Ride

Kenji Takezo does not have the gift of vision
Except that in whatever he does see
He sees a wave. So when he walks
His way to school, he is surfing.

The row of houses surge into a wall of water.
He dodges the eaves crashing behind him,
Then ducks under the overhang of a tree,
The falling crest of a Pipeline breaker.

He stands beneath the shade where he hears
The hollow music inside the tube,
The green leaves shimmying like the ocean
Turning itself around him.

He exits the ceiling of foliage to outrun
The whitewash of cars chasing him.
Morning commuters showing all teeth and eyes.
Their blaring horns, fellow surfers cheering him on.

In this way, he surfs always.
His whole life, the longest ride,
The perfect wave in the ocean for which
He searches endlessly and never finds.

∎TWO

▌ His First Big Surf

The day he makes the paddle
Out into the ocean that divides
The men from boys
Kenji Takezo feels the pulse of the Pacific
Enter him,
A reunion of familiar elements,
The water from which he was made.

But when he goes to ride,
The wave behaves like the older surfers,
The locals of the beach,
Who often pick him up by the ankles
Then vigorously shake free
The loose coins from Kenji's pockets.
Even though they steal
His money for lunch
And drop him on his head,
He welcomes the sting of rushing water,
The pain of becoming a man.

▌ After Kenji Takezo's Worst Wipeout
He Takes Home with Him Some Ocean

The wave holds him too long
Not the embrace a worried mother gives
Her found child
But the dreaded scissor grip of a masked wrestler
Going for the pin, legs squeezed tight
So his opponent cannot breathe.
Before the referee slaps
His hand ten times against the sand,
Kenji, unable to escape the locked crotch,
Makes his body limp, plays dead.

He then gathers all his strength,
All the life in him, and with one
Big convulsion, the spirit spiking him,
He breaks free from the grasp.
When he surfaces, he inhales deeply
Air and sea together.
His nose stings,
A mob of bees swarming inside.

The rest of the day, it feels like that,
A sneeze that won't come out.
He is compelled to impersonate
Jimmy Durante and does it badly.
The force of water swelling in his sinus,
Tension builds around his eyes.
In an effort to coax the sneeze, he tickles
His nostrils, sniffs pepper. Nothing.

His brother the bodybuilder knows a remedy.
He has Kenji wear over his head a paper bag
Tells him to breathe deeply.

When Kenji cannot see
The brother lifts him,
The perfect weight, into the air.
The sudden jerk and pull releases the pressure.
A wave spills from Kenji's nose
Breaking on his brother who does not know
How to swim.

No, I am not deformed.
I wear these socks
Because I haven't any gloves,
And my fingers are bitten with frost.
They feel like stumps.
Luckily, I finished covering
The citrus tree with sheets of burlap.
Before darkness,
I will light a smudge pot
Near the mummified trunk,
Then anoint my hands in a blue salve.
Yesterday was cold
But the freeze is on now.
I must remind myself
Not to lick any cars.
Mr. Nishizawa, a house over,
Told me his nephew
Lost a fourth of his tongue
For that reason. Years ago,
The rosebushes were ruined to a freeze
And have never come back.
If needed, I will stay up all night
And pray, will let the hoarfrost
Burn in my chest. My grandfather
Ate the yield from this tree
After he died. I saw him.

The three-story wave,
Kenji Takezo knows, he cannot ride.
It is too large to hold
Its own shape,
The way a cumulus cloud
Shifts in unstable air.
Fifteen minutes to get to school,
He stands up on the wave anyway.
His feet missing
The board completely.
He tiptoes the surface
Until the whitewash tackles him
Hard. He crashes to the sand floor
Where the Pacific sits
On his belly. It is much heavier
Than the brother, a whole year older,
Who often pins his shoulders
And dangles over his face
A thick wad of milk spit.

Kenji has to say the two words
His brother types
Repeatedly into his chest,
Keys the size of fists.
He has to say
The words that give
Complete liberation
Just by saying it.
But by saying it,
His brother becomes
The victor. The ocean
Pounding on his chest,

The oldest brother now.
Kenji shouts over and again,
Monkey's uncle, monkey's uncle,
Until the weight is lifted.

That boy, the champion breath holder,
Kenji Takezo, lost his title
This year to Mack Stanton
A retired truck driver
New to the area.
Held in the town swimming pool
Thirty-five participants inhaled
Deeply all at once
Submerged the depth.
The contest went on into twilight.
One by one each person
Came up sucking air.
Kenji was the town favorite.
We wanted him to win again.
He trained so hard,
It was the only real talent
He had
Other than surfing and making
Trouble. When he surfaced
Second to last
Gulping the night
Then vomiting water,
We were disappointed.
He was doing so well.
He had his lucky twenty-pound brick
Cradled in his lap.
It kept him down.
But that trucker Mack was too good.
He read
Comic books, aloud, underwater.
We watched from the bleachers

His laughter bursting above him.
Kenji saw this too.
He never had anybody
Read to him
Not even his mother,
And he wanted to hear
What was being read
What his opponent found so funny.

▌Kenji Takezo Learns to Keep
His Mouth Closed

He eats so much sand
After he wipes out on a wave,
No water under it,
That the quickness in his step
All of a sudden slows.
When Kenji paddles out again
He goes to stand, to ride another breaker,
But this time his ability to jump swiftly
One motion to his feet from a lying position
Almost fails. He stumbles.
His footing becomes too wide,
The measured foundation of a statue
Feet planted far enough to hold
The extra pounds of stone,
The round sky heavy on Atlas's back.
Straining to keep his balance,
Kenji rides the wave straight in
A constipated look on his face.

He beaches himself, the sun baking
The heaviness inside his belly.
It hardens until he cannot move.
His mind taken over,
Clogged by thoughts of quartz and feldspar.
Kenji lay in the shorebreak
Waiting for the surf to smash
Him into a thousand tiny pieces.

▍The Shirt His Father Wore That Day
Was Wrinkled, Slightly

It is a stunt
Kenji Takezo finds himself
Performing unexpectedly.
The rhythm of the Pacific in his feet,
He leaps
Onto the ironing board
His mother is getting ready
To straighten his father's
Work clothes, the creases
After a good washing.

Kenji takes a stance
Wide enough to support
His center of gravity,
Flexes his knees
Counterbalancing the instability
Of water, his arms
Apart for symmetry.

He watches
The crest of a wave
Pitch over and enclose him,
Hears in the chamber
The silent pulse of its heart.
As the walls close in,
Kenji crouches lower,
Leans forward to escape
The collapsing ocean.

The ironing table floats
The small boy
Only for a moment.

Too much weight in front, it purls
Nose-first, into thick
Brown shag.
His mother, bringing the cold
Iron and a bundle of laundry,
Sees just in time
Kenji diving into the deep
Cushion of their couch.

When he surfaces,
Her expression is one
He has never seen,
One that is completely new
To the muscles in her face.

Kenji has broken
Her favorite ironing table—
A wedding gift from the Yamaguchis.
The legs, split beyond
Their crotch.

His mother on her knees
Tries to iron on the ruined table
Anyway. His father needs
A shirt to impress
The same co-workers
He sees daily.
In this posture, his mother's movements
Remind Kenji of a surfer
Waxing the board she will ride.

▌Black with Red Spots

The remains of a monsoon
Are ashes
Riding the deep sky.
The gully quickens with floodwater.
I can't remember
The girl's name.
I swam, mid-January,
Across the aqueduct
To impress her.
She laughed at my expression
When I broke
The calm
Surface of winter.
I went home
Skin steel blue
A severe case of pneumonia.
The exquisite frogs I saw
During a fever, lost
To nightmares. Mushrooms
Bloom in this humidity.
At first light, I'll watch
My shadow
Twist in morning silence.
She brought a sack
Round pears
Gathered, prematurely,
From her aunt's orchard
Plagued with fire blight.
I didn't say, but the one I had
Was sour,
Ten seeds in its core!
I missed a month of school.
The following year,

She moved. Wind chimes,
Suspended off the metal awning,
Are still.
Her name, it started with an *L*.

Inside the empty chamber of a wave is the same
Sound a child memorizes
Hiding, dusk, in the green heaven above
His house. Madness calming
The sky while a slight offshore breeze gives
Breath to a paper wind carp.
Hungry, its aperture is round, the letter *O,*
Open the way a folding comber forms a mouth.

The parents of that child sip a bitter tea.
Their lips tight, they wonder why
He sits so often in the puzzle elm—
Never fitting the pieces together.
He's lost in concentration
Riding the ocean he remembers, feels
Surging through his veins,
Currents from a ground swell miles away.

Through a back window, he sees
The two in the living room watching television.
Silence resting between them.
Their thoughts washed by the drone of voices.
When the streetlamps flicker on
The son climbs out of the tree,
Returns home. His mother has fixed for him
A scoop of orange sorbet.

He lets it stay in the blue ceramic bowl.

From Rooftops, Kenji Takezo Throws Himself

Be prepared.
—Boy Scout motto

In midair, he hesitates at the moment
Gravity begins its pull. Before closing
His eyes, he peeks at the earth
Spinning below him, wonders why
When he jumps into space
The planet never abandons him.

The trick, he must remember, is in the landing:
Keep his face and genitals out of it.
Adjusting himself in the air,
He arches his back and bends
His flailing arms and legs behind,
A broken swan plunging from the ten-foot heavens.
When he smacks the cool cement
Belly first, his heart bounces. Still, he holds
The wind, usually, inside him.

A year ago the ocean rose
Six feet before it turned and collapsed.
Tackled firmly, he saw nothing but white.
His belly slapped the sand.
His breath knocked free. Ten minutes
He struggled, floating without
Weight, until it was recovered
Safely from the grip of water.

To be certain he never again fumbles
The breath he has kept since birth,
He rehearses the vertical flight
Every day, making his stomach strong.
Next week he will start

Leaping off two- and three-story buildings
Preparing for the wipeouts he will take
When he falls from waves
The size of cathedrals.

Washed with volcanic cinder,
The end of sunset is a deep mauve.
It's the summer solstice,
And Havaiya, who knows this,
The longest day of the year,
Attempts to somersault
The entire grass knoll.
At the top, a metal structure:
Rusted hood and two side panels
Of a late Toyota
Twisted into a filly
Laid out on the night road.
The lawn, pressing Havaiya's skin,
Is cooling.
After five revolutions,
She stops
Dizzy. The world, a crazy place,
Spins around her. She completes
Five more. Stops. Her parents,
Watching darkness
Overcome the heavens
Behind the curves of a horse,
Have forgotten her.
This was the sky, the day
They met: hills, surrounding
The city, active with fire.
Early next dawn,
The sky was ultramarine,
A thin membrane of ash
Lifting the ground.
Havaiya's halfway to the flats
When they remember.
She's sick with laughter
Listening to her own heart.

Cold, the water,
Enough to cause the gravity to reverse
Between Kenji Takezo's legs,
His testicles hide
Inside the woman in him,
While he pulls on his wetsuit.
Through the neoprene bubbles he feels
Himself not all
There like the action figure Big Jim
Handsome yet no sex when you check.
In the surf, he expels
The urine his body heated.
Seeping between two skins, it keeps him warm
Until the ocean flushes through him.

▌The Ocean Inside Him

After Kenji Takezo fell from a wave,
The turbulence of whitewash confused
His sense of direction.
He breathed in
When he should have

Held tight. By accident, he swallowed
The Pacific. The water poured down his throat,
A blue cascade he could not see.
He felt in his stomach
The heavy life of the ocean.

It wasn't funny, but he giggled
When a school of fish tickled his ribs.
He went home, the surf not rideable,
It was no longer there,
The water weighted in his belly.

That night, while he slept, the tide moved.
The long arms of the moon
Reached inside him pulling the Pacific free.
When he woke the next morning,
He lay in a puddle of ocean that was his.

That dude, that surfer guy, he's crazy.
I saw him
While I was walking down Pacific Coast Highway.
He was on the bus.
No, on top of the bus.
He was standing barefoot on the roof.
His legs bent and his arms out,
He somehow kept his balance.

The driver had no idea. He didn't know.
He kept accelerating
Unaware he had an extra passenger.
The big green bus sped at least forty miles an hour,
And that crazy surfer guy
He started walking toward the front,
Placing foot over foot until he reached
The edge where he stopped to hang
Ten toes just above the driver's head.
And the driver still didn't see!

That surfer guy, he was a hood ornament
Guiding the long bus through traffic.
The asphalt rushing beneath him.
He was so smooth and had such style.
He folded his arms behind him,
Arched his back in a pose
That showed he was full of grace.
Even when the bus slowed
Then stopped to pick up more passengers,
He never lost his composure.

I watched him go three blocks
Until he drifted off in the current of cars.

∎THREE

▌ The Witch of Miyajima That the
First Squad Encountered, Circa 1470

We saw her from behind
As we cut through the forest
Today at late dawn.
She was standing upright in the river.
The three of us
Foot soldiers of the Lord Shimazu.
We were returning to the castle
After securing the land
For the lord's morning ride.
The air was calm as usual.

She was fleeing back and forth
Across the quiet rushes
Riding a slat of black oak.
Her garments were torn.
We were astonished at the sight
Her evil conjuring on water.

We concealed ourselves in a tall juniper
Afraid she would throw a spell,
If she saw us
Turn us into snakes.
When finally she steered herself
To shore,
We leapt out of hiding.
Takara-san took a stone and bashed
The back of her head,
A sun rose on her demon-white hair
The length of winter. Before she collapsed
Iwasaki-san and I lashed with our swords

Deep into her body.
She dropped to earth
Imitating a willow struck by lightning.

This morning we slew the hag,
Dismantled her
Brought the ugly head for the lord,
And left the limbs to worms.
Each of us,
Splattered with her
Poisoned blood,
Bathed in the river. The sharp water
Embraced us.

▌ The Widow Who Was Slaughtered

I saw the murder of Shibasaki-san.
I was on my way
Walking upriver to watch her
Ride the quick current.
She was there every morning
Floating on the rapid that curls
Back on itself.
She stood on the washboard
Her late husband carved
Out of the driftwood he found
Trapped in the same rapid she rode.

Shibasaki-san that day,
When she saw me approaching,
Maneuvered herself to the shallows.
She was always delighted to see me.
I often brought for her
Vegetables from big sister's garden.
She was teaching me
How to ride the current,
How to turn and control
The board with my feet.

When three soldiers
Jumped out of a bush
And attacked Shibasaki-san,
I dropped into the rushes
A basket of red carrots.
They slashed at her with swords,
The shiniest I've ever seen.
I ran home,

Didn't tell anyone, not even
Mama or Papa.
Nobody could know I saw
What happened.
They will come for me.

▌FOUR

▮ Lost Under the Ocean After Falling Off a Wave

for Tito and not for Tito

His air was not his air.

And so Kenji Takezo's breath was not his breath

Underwater, not the breath

He drew before he was taken

Deep, the ocean's fist driving him

There and leaving without

Showing him how to get back,

His brother ditching him at the market.

He stood alone in the pet supply aisle

Where nobody went, nobody would find him.

The exit not where he thought.

He had to make

His own route, find for himself the surface

And hurry, even he, a champion

Breath holder could not keep his breath that long.

Up and down, two paths only,

He had to choose one and went.

Short and choppy, his strokes were not his strokes

But those belonging to panic.

The air he took in becoming quickly

The carbon dioxide swelling in his lungs, the way

When he inhaled pot, it expanded, burned.

He longed to cough, but couldn't.

He had to hold it in,

His friends said so.

Where he went, he did not go.

The buoyancy made him

Stay in place. He wished he had

The weight to sink him,

So that he would know

The opposite way was up
But his head was too light and he floated.
Not enough oxygen in his brain,
His mind was empty,
Heavy thoughts disappearing in thin air.

In his chest, the carbon dioxide erupted
Forcing him to exhale
A cloud of restless bubbles
That tickled his belly, his knees, his toes
As they dashed away from him.
No breath, he turned
Himself around and chased after them
Until he popped at the surface.

Inside an eight-foot wave, Kenji Takezo stands.
Arms outstretched for symmetry,
Feet gripping the board, he holds himself
With simple poise and commands
The ocean spinning around him.
Green water forming an empty chamber,
A sanctum all his.
No brother with whom to share it.

Throughout their whole childhoods,
Kenji and his older brother,
Joe, had to split
A bedroom. Divided down the middle,
The imaginary line became, for Kenji,
Very real. He learned early
The meaning of No Trespassing.
On one side, his side, he was safe.
But if he stepped on the other half,
Even by the easy mistake of using
The door, Joe would plunge
Down on Kenji with the strength of a winter wave.
He kept him quelled with one arm
Bent around his neck choking him.
With this grasp, which he learned
Watching costumed wrestlers on television,
Joe would thrust into Kenji's mouth
A sweatsock
Soiled from a day's wear.

Too often, pinned against the floor,
Head locked in the crook of Joe's arm,

Kenji, forced to chew the dirty whites
Five times, held his breath
So not to taste
The flavor of his brother's sour foot.

▌ His Wave

The retired man showed the town
The perfect wave
He kept
Inside a bottle.
He turned it continually
Back on itself so the water
Broke over and again, never resting.
He told also
The story
How it was captured.
All at no cost.
With each telling the wave
Grew big then bigger
Until finally it no longer fit.
He had to buy large and larger
Bottles that would hold
His growing wave.
When it became too big
And he could find no bottle
To store it, he had a tank
Installed in the yard.
Now when he tells of its capture
Nobody believes him.
Now he is the town's
Crazy man
Who spends too much time,
Gets too much sun
Next to the swimming pool
He never swims in.

▌The Kite a Man Made

A man flies
Above the city trees
His father's good shirt.
Hung over
A thin cross of wood dowel,
It is buttoned to the neck,
And tied at the waist.
The wind is dry.
Another kite appears.
It's an old fedora.
Instantly, a dogfight
Breaks out. The hat
Striking the chest
Knocks breath from the shirt,
Goes for an arm,
But is batted away.
Strings snarl.
For a moment, the man loses
Control. He recovers,
Jerks his spool,
Snapping the fedora's line.
It's been five years,
The man realizes,
Since he's seen
His father so alive.

▌Kenji Takezo Becomes Water

The ocean with its large mouth swallowed him.
One bite, and very little chewing.
He balled up his body
As he sank into the belly,
Where the water waited to digest him.

He held himself together, his air
Kept tight, but the gas in his lungs began to expand.
It was choking
Him. He was choking himself.
So he gave up fighting back his breath,
His bubbles rose to the heavens.

The ocean burped,
A small disturbance on the surface.

Kenji relaxed his body, emptied
His thoughts into the element.
He became the ocean,
His mind and body floating with the current.
He no longer had to breathe.
When he opened his eyes,
He saw himself,
The deep blueness spanning the planet.

▌ Autumn Heat

Incoming tide climbs high
Against the damp rocks;
Crabs and starfish
Bed down. Near the harbor mouth,
A slow, twisting, blue light
Warns boaters
Away from the dark jetty.
Out of the sky, ash and cinder fall
Kissing my face.
I think, at first, rain has begun.
But no storm clouds
Cover the night's full red moon.
I decide it is the salt mist.

Engineers in the late fifties
Set damaged trolleys
A mile out on the ocean floor, to stall
The progress of Aleutian swells
That pummel the oil refineries.
One winter a guy named Max Medeiros
Paddled a nine-foot longboard
Through the harbor and surfed
A giant breaker
At the deep water reef
Called "cable cars."
The whitewash, four times overhead,
Plunged down on him.
The board washed ashore
The next day in pieces.

Near midchannel, a splash.
Mackerel chase mullets
Into the warm air. It reminds me
I must return home.

Under the light of streetlamps,
I am smeared in blackness.
The deejay on the car radio
Announces a fire
Burning in the foothills since noon.

At sea, the light still turning, blue.

▌Orchards

His father owned the town
Bowling alley, and brought home
Balls no longer usable.
Hoping to find for them
Some other use, he would say,
I just can't throw them out.
He set them in the yard
Behind the house
Where the grass grew
High above their round bodies,
But died underneath.
The finger holes
Alive with spiders.

One winter, when a freeze
Destroyed their tall lawn,
They saw
How many were there.
The polished black orbs,
Fruit of imaginary trees.

▌His Brother Surfing

He lost in the surf his composure.
Unlike his balanced life on land,
Where his polished manner kept him poised,
Joe Takezo in the ocean had no style.
When he paddled, he grabbed too much
Water, pulled with too much muscle.
Joe's thick arms cut the ocean quick,
Not the long pulls of a lone sculler
Who glides across the morning surface
With the graceful motions of a sea insect.
Instead, his short, choppy strokes moved him
Barely, not enough to float
Over the big sets that broke outside the lineup.
Most often, his confidence was crushed
By the ocean that fell in the impact zone.

When Joe did catch a wave
And when he did get to his feet,
He struggled,
An aneurism victim relearning how to walk,
Mixed signals from the brain.
Joe's legs were those of a stick figure,
Who stands perfectly straight
No confidence in the foundation,
No bounce in his knees.
His toes gripped the board tightly,
The balls planted firmly,
So he could hold himself. His stance,
He established low,
A center of gravity wide enough to lift
Three hundred pounds over his head.

But no matter how strong Joe was,
No matter how sturdy his foothold,

When he rode a wave,
The surge of water threw him
Off balance. He had to flail
His arms in tight,
Backward circles attempting to regain
The stability he lost in the water, never had.

▌ His First Dance

Kenji Takezo feels without warning
The music of the affair
Enter him,
But he doesn't know
How to dance.
The surge of energy,
A hundred pins of sleep,
Pricking his soles.
He does the only thing
He can do as the girl
To whom he is speaking
Rises in the manner of a wave.
He surfs.
It is an involuntary response
To stand on his board,
This dance floor.
He controls the balance,
Which is everything
The best he can,
His feet not bare
The way he is used to.

He keeps an eye on his partner,
The girl whose movements are unsteady.
Together they create
The dance. The crowd forms
Another wave, he sees it
And he rides calmly through
The wall of their bodies.
When he escapes
The tube of their arms,
The falling crest,
All he can hear
Breaking around him is the applause
Of water.

▌October, Remembering the Ride No One Saw

Steel horses nodding
In the petroleum field are beasts
That suck
The crude of earth.
They have lived here for as long as I
Remember. This moment,

I smell wild incense:
Heather, abducted by a desert wind.
Its growth hides
The rain-carved ribs of the foothills.
Evening swallows
The city fasting on late fall.

Years ago, after hearing the story
About a boy who lost
Both legs while playing on an oil pump,
I was dared to straddle one.
All my friends were there to watch
The Pacific behind me burning with dusk.

The brute lifted me to the sky,
Where I merged with the twilight,
A warm breeze embracing my back.
None of them noticed
The world stopped to breathe.
When I looked, they disappeared.

Nearby in pink-flowered bushes
Someone found
The girl who'd been missing for weeks.
They stood in awe, the body
Decomposing, while I rode
The slow bucking animal.

Two months later, off the same pump,
A man dove,
An imperfect swan into night.
He landed in the dirt gully
Breaking the soft, white wings
He never had.

Today, I catch in my hand
An insect charged with lightning.
It tickles
The obscure scoop of my palm
As I hold it to my mouth and explain
A wish so simple

By morning I will have forgotten it.
I release
The bug to a desert wind
That is racing toward the sea,
A brutal dryness in its wake.
Fire in the hills everywhere.

I am trying to stop
What is happening: lying here
The usual field of golden poppies.

A small boy
Controls a red box kite
Pacing across a cloudless sky.

It has happened before.

His mother and sister
Sit cross-legged
Watching from the knoll.

I know what's coming.
The boy, running, will trip,
The spool of string
Slipping from his hands—
The box kite
Nose dives toward earth.

Seeing that he is unhurt,
The sister and mother
Will hysterically laugh.

It is about to happen any time now.

▌Kenji Takezo the Surfer
Who Can Dance, Too

Last night at the dance
I never saw anything like it.
That guy, that surfer
Kenji Takezo went crazy
Prancing here and there.
He was all over the place.
Everybody stopped to watch him
Sweep across the floor.
He hopped onto tables,
Ran up the walls.
We applauded him, the moves
Only he could do.
When he poured the punch bowl
Over his own head,
We cheered him.
He shook it out of his hair
Like red ocean.
He zipped through the crowd.
Some people
Kept trying to trip him.
They wanted to see Kenji
Fall, go down humiliated.
They wanted to take the attention
Away from him.
But his balance was too good.
He never lost his footing.

▋ The Old-Timer Who Told Himself Away

He was there to see every morning
If the surf was up.
But the waves he found were never
Big enough for him to ride.
They were not the size
He needed, did not have
The strength to move him,
The ocean of beer solid in his belly.

Instead the old-timer recounted his tale
All the time to everybody
Who would listen.
Kenji Takezo was one of them.
It became part of his routine.
While Kenji waxed his board
He would listen to the story, that day
The old-timer rode twenty years ago.

Over and again it was the same.
Except with each telling
The old-timer gave a little more
Height to the waves and so the tale
Flourished. When Kenji first heard it,
The day was big, the waves ceiling high.
Then, when he heard it a second time,
It was the biggest of the season, one-story tall.
After that, two stories, three,
The biggest day of the year.

Each occasion the old-timer told the tale,

The surf grew, kept growing big, bigger,

Huge while he, in comparison,

Shrunk, got smaller.

The waves finally became so gigantic, the biggest in decades,

That the old-timer, riding

Alongside the walls, was dwarfed.

He became tiny.

The next morning, Kenji waxed

His board and waited for him,

The old-timer, who never appeared to tell about the biggest day ever.

▌Kenji Takezo Fights Back

He takes the biggest bite he can
Out of the shark
That knocked him off his board
Making him miss
The best wave of the day.

The shark, staggers, can't believe
It is bit, a chunk gone from his dorsal fin.
No longer can he slice
Just below the surface to show
The beachgoers his foreboding sharkhood,
Fifteen inches of triangular might.
Now, he is an embarrassment.
The other sharks will see
How he failed to uphold his duty
The image of the shark as terror.
They will laugh.
He is not the graceful machine of nature.
He has to avenge himself
So he goes after the surfer Kenji again.

Urging it on, Kenji
Submerges the depths and secures his stance,
Feet planted deep in the sand bottom.
He feels the burrowing crabs tickle
His soles still tender from the late spring.
When the shark comes for him,
Its eyes closed to life,
Kenji fakes left and moves right
To avoid its gaping mouth. He tackles it.
They fall to the floor wrestling in a cloud of bubbles.
In the confusion, Kenji ties up
Its tail, a knot he learned in the Boy Scouts.

He then places it in a headlock.
As Kenji tightens his grip, the vice,
Giving it the sleeper hold
The shark goes limp
Allowing Kenji to take another big bite.

In disbelief, the shark stops swimming,
Momentarily, to brush itself off, review
The situation. Two mouthfuls missing from its fin.
A target now for ruffian harbor seals
Who will snicker, maybe
Gang up and beat the second-rate foe.
Its reputation wrecked,
The shark swims away with its fin down.

▌He Knows Not Every Ride Is Perfect

Kenji falls but never
Strikes earth,
The ocean always,
The water, a safety net,
But it isn't that safe,
It stops him
But it also stops him
From breathing.
In order to save the air
He holds, Kenji keeps
His thoughts
From becoming words
Too heavy, the weight
He cannot carry
Not even in the gravity
Under water.

He lets his body go limber,
Exhales bubbles
Empty of thought.
The thrashing he accepts,
He deserves it
Trying to stand
On water
Charged with a thousand
Miles of anger.

Grateful acknowledgment is made to the following publications in which some of the poems in this collections first appeared: *Bamboo Ridge* ("When for Weeks the Sea Is Flat") and *The Quarterly* ("Orchards"). Grateful acknowledgment is also made to Pearl Press for the chapbook *The Wave He Caught,* in which a number of these poems first appeared.

Elizabeth M. Larson

ABOUT THE AUTHOR

Rick Noguchi was born in Los Angeles in 1967 and
raised in Culver City. He holds a B.A. in English from
California State University, Long Beach, and an M.F.A.
in creative writing from Arizona State University. *The
Ocean Inside Kenji Takezo* is his first collection of poems
and is winner of the 1995 Associated Writing Programs'
award series in poetry. His chapbook, *The Wave He
Caught,* won the 1994 Pearl Editions Prize.

Library of Congress Cataloging-in Publication Data

Noguchi, Rick

    The ocean inside Kenji Takezo / Rick Noguchi.

      p. cm. — (Pitt poetry series)

    ISBN 0-8229-3959-2 (alk. paper). — ISBN 0-8229-5613-6

(pbk. : alk. paper)

    I. Title.   II Series

PS3564.0353029   1996   96-10143